Raptors

TOON TELLEGEN was born in 1941 on one of the islands in the south-west of the Netherlands. He is one of the best-known Dutch writers, with a long list of awards to his name. In 2007 he received two major prizes for his entire oeuvre. He considers himself in the first place a poet and has published more than twenty collections of poetry to date, but he is also a novelist and a prolific and popular children's author. Toon Tellegen lives in Amsterdam with his wife, and worked as a GP until his recent retirement. He gives frequent readings of his work, often with musical accompaniment; in 2009 he read the whole of *Raafvogels* ('Raptors') at the Perdu theatre in Amsterdam.

JUDITH WILKINSON is a British poet and prize-winning translator living in the Netherlands. Her first two collections of translations, the Belgian poet Miriam Van hee's *Instead of Silence* (a PBS Recommendation), and Toon Tellegen's *About Love and About Nothing Else*, were published by Shoestring Press. A collection of her own poems, *Tightrope Dancer*, was published by Shoestring Press in 2010. Some of these poems have been performed by the dance theatre company The Kosh. Her website can be visited at www.judithwilkinson.net.

T0099109

'Family life can be unbearable. Yet for all manner of reasons, we continue to tolerate it.' This might be the message of Toon Tellegen's poignant yet hilarious depictions of his own family, especially of 'my father, my paltry father, my little Goliath', whose character so dominates this witty and profound collection.

Robert Minhinnick

TOON TELLEGEN

Raptors

Translated with an introduction by
JUDITH WILKINSON

CARCANET

First published in Great Britain in 2011 by
Carcanet Press Limited
Alliance House
Cross Street
Manchester M2 7AQ

Raafvogels first published in the Netherlands in 2006 by
Em. Querido's Uitgeverij B.V.,
Singel 262, 1016 AC Amsterdam, The Netherlands

Copyright © 2006 by Toon Tellegen, Amsterdam, Em. Querido's Uitgeverij B.V.

Translation copyright © Judith Wilkinson 2011

The right of Toon Tellegen to be identified as the author of this work
has been asserted by him in accordance with the
Copyright, Designs and Patents Act of 1988

The right of Judith Wilkinson to be identified as the translator of this work
has been asserted by her in accordance with the
Copyright, Designs and Patents Act of 1988

A CIP catalogue record for this book is available from the British Library

ISBN 978 1 84777 083 7

This book was published with the support of the
Dutch Foundation for Literature

N ederlands
letterenfonds
dutch foundation
for literature

The publisher acknowledges financial assistance from Arts Council England

Typeset by XL Publishing Services, Tiverton

Contents

II

III

Acknowledgements

Poems included in this collection have appeared in the following journals:

Agenda, Carapace, Equinox, De Hoffeskrant, The Journal, The Manhattan Review, Orbis, PN Review, Poetry Ireland Review, Poetry Review, Poetry Salzburg Review, The Seventh Quarry, Stand and *Tzum*.

The poem 'My father/got under the skin' appeared in the poetry section of www.languageandculture.net.

The poem 'My father/was immense and limitless' was nominated for a Pushcart Prize in 2008 by *The Manhattan Review*.

The poem 'My father/there was a gaping hole in him' won joint fourth prize in the *Orbis* Readers Award in 2009.

I am grateful to Toon Tellegen for his detailed scrutiny of the translations and for his comments and suggestions.

I would like to thank my parents and my brother Michael Wilkinson for their input, and Anthony Runia and Geni Fitzgerald for some useful suggestions.

I am enormously grateful to The Dutch Foundation for Literature for a translation grant.

Thanks also to Toon Tellegen's publisher, Em. Querido's Uitgeverij B.V., for permission to print this translation of Toon Tellegen's collection *Raafvogels,* which was published in 2006 in Amsterdam.

Introduction

Toon Tellegen was born in 1941 in the town of Brielle, in the south-west of the Netherlands. He grew up in a family of four whose father was a GP. Tellegen later studied medicine himself, and spent some years working in a hospital in Kenya. Eventually he settled in Amsterdam, where he lives with his wife and where, until quite recently, he too worked as a GP. Tellegen's earliest affinity was with poetry and he considers himself primarily a poet. Later, he also began to publish children's stories, originally created for his own children, as well as novels for adults, plays, and a semi-fictional memoir of his maternal grandfather. Tellegen frequently gives readings of his work, often with musical accompaniment; in 2009 he read the whole of *Raafvogels* ('Raptors') – to a full house – at Amsterdam's Perdu theatre.

His grandfather, who had spent the first half of his life in Russia, appears to have had an important impact on Tellegen's childhood. Not only did he instil in Tellegen a love of Russian literature, but he was also an inexhaustible source of fantastical stories. This may go some way towards explaining Tellegen's own unorthodox style of storytelling and his tragicomic approach to his subject matter. Not surprisingly, Tellegen has been likened to writers like Bulgakov or the Russian absurd writer Daniil Charms.

In the Netherlands Tellegen is practically a household name. The extent of his work is astonishing, ranging from his enchanting, quietly philosophical children's books – enjoyed by children and adults alike – to his other prose works, as well as more than twenty collections of poetry to date. He has won many major prizes, including two recent awards for his entire oeuvre. If anything, his work seems to have been gathering momentum and resonance, as he constantly experiments with new forms and techniques. Outside the Netherlands, his reputation is growing as his work is beginning to appear in translation. In Britain, an opera, *The Cricket Recovers*, based on Tellegen's children's stories, was performed in 2005 at the Aldeburgh Festival and later at the Almeida Theatre in London. Boxer Books has published a number of Tellegen's children's books. *Raptors* is the second collection of his poetry to appear in Britain.

Tellegen has spoken of the poems in *Raptors* as improvisations on a theme, the theme of 'My father', adding that, as in jazz, there seemed infinite scope for further improvisation, further changes too. He felt he could have continued improvising on 'raptors' indefinitely. Even for a writer who is constantly reinventing himself as Tellegen does, *Raptors* was a startlingly fresh departure. It is as if its subject matter were an explosive source of energy. The book has been hailed as one of the highpoints of his oeuvre.

Tellegen has always been at home with the sequence form, but the poems in this, his longest, work well on their own, too. Cumulatively, they build a tragicomic picture of an extravagantly dysfunctional family, each poem except the last beginning ritualistically with the words 'My father'. Tellegen's approach to his subject matter is, as always, unconventional: without filling in details about the characters' lives, without a plot, without carefully setting the scene, each poem plunges in with a saying or an idiom that sums up some aspect of the father's nature. There are no gentle shifts, no gradual unfoldings: each verse is a new leap, a new moment of creation. Discussing Tellegen's collection *About Love and About Nothing Else* in *The Manhattan Review*, the American poet and critic John Brehm commented on this originality in Tellegen's poetry: 'it is hard to overstate his uniqueness'. Brehm emphasises Tellegen's 'diagnostic curiosity about the human condition', arguing that 'it is a fallen world Tellegen's poems take place in, a world of painful absurdities where we are free to explore the many ways we are trapped; a world where abstractions stalk the earth'.

The Dutch poet and critic Tom van Deel has remarked that Tellegen often needs some kind of linguistic agreement with himself regarding the shape of a sequence: he frequently relies on a recurrent opening phrase or verbal pattern that forms the catalyst of the writing process or an anchor for his imagination. Each poem of his collection *In N*, for instance, set in the imaginary place 'N.', begins with the words 'In N.'. Van Deel points out how effective this mode of writing is in *Raptors*. In beginning each poem with an idiom or proverb that evokes something of the father's make-up and temperament, Tellegen taps into the lifeblood of language, while at the same time offsetting the father's reveries and exalted conceits with something altogether more mundane and earthy. Other critics have commented on *Raptors*' peculiar mixing of everyday, domestic imagery with surreal description ('my father flew away', 'he climbed into a vase'), and the piling up of abstractions that seem to clash and bounce off each other ('gluttony and shabbiness', 'simplicity and ambivalence'). It is as if the language itself – restless, hyperbolical – has been infected by the picture that is portrayed. And yet the poems do not spin off into chaos, for there is always a logic, a psychological coherence, that holds them together.

The world in which the characters interact in *Raptors* is contorted. Nature itself has become chaotic, discordant: it is a place where 'sparrows howled, swallows blared', or where 'magpies screeched in overwhelming sycamores'. The father, with his ominous, manic energy, dominates all those round him. His grandiosity, his constitutional hubris, his wild flights of fancy, coupled with a consummate neediness, slowly drain the life out of his family. And he remains profoundly unaware of his impact on others: see, for instance, the poem 'My father/slept through unrest and sorrow', where sleep seems to have become a metaphor for a kind of wilful unconsciousness. The whole family is, as it were, held hostage, a prey to the father's whims and fluctuating moods. Gradually one sees how the sons, starved of attention and consistently upstaged by their father, are torn between 'saving' and abandoning their father, and in the course of the book their frustration mounts. The mother, once 'young and luxuriant', becomes 'scrawny and mute', exhausted bit by bit in her efforts to support her husband and bear his melodramatic outbursts ('my mother slowly slept her way downstream/from upland plains'). With great psychological insight the whole dynamics of this family is exposed; each in turn unleashes some measure of cruelty on the other. And yet the picture painted is still compassionate, and the narrator is not without empathy.

The translations of the poems in the sequence evolved over a period of about a year, in close consultation with Toon Tellegen. His queries and suggestions made for much rethinking and discussion. He encouraged me to take liberties in order to preserve the strangeness and rawness of the language, which at times is almost breaking at the seams, and he drew comparisons with Francis Bacon's work and the distortion used in his portraits. Occasionally, where Tellegen was in retrospect slightly dissatisfied with the Dutch, he asked me to make a few minor changes. Among other things, this involved changing the layout and thereby shortening two of the poems. I tried to keep the English as idiomatic as the Dutch and to find English proverbs and expressions that matched the Dutch as much as possible. Surprisingly often, a match existed, or at least a close equivalent, but where there was no real equivalent

I looked for solutions that allowed for a similar play on imagery as in the Dutch.

In *Raptors* we see an artist at the height of his powers. Using minimal brushstrokes and a large canvas, Tellegen gives us this complex portrait of a family, in language that is tantalisingly apt, tantalisingly strange.

Judith Wilkinson

Raptors

Preface

Years ago I invented someone whom I called my father.

It was morning, very early, I couldn't sleep any more, I remember it quite clearly.

My father didn't seem surprised at having suddenly appeared out of nowhere and, in his turn, invented my mother, my brothers and myself. He even, that very same morning, invented the life we should lead.

We led that life for a long time. My father made sure that there was always something inadequate about it, something painful, like a shoe that pinches.

Sometimes he would take us out for a walk. He would walk ahead of us, look around, accost passers-by and say something like: 'I give the friendless a home. What do you do?'

The passers-by would shrug their shoulders and walk on. They didn't have the faintest idea what it was they did.

One day he lost his balance, fell awkwardly and landed in a ditch.

My brothers pulled him out. My mother wiped the duckweed off his face.

'Why did you have to invent me?' he said to me, looking at me in a way I have never been able to describe properly.

That evening he asked me to invent an incurable illness for him, one that would take possession of him very quickly. As it grew light, he died.

After he had died, my mother asked my brothers to join her in the room.

'You must forget him,' she said.

I was standing in the corridor and looked in through the keyhole.

'Right away?' my brothers asked.

'The sooner the better,' my mother said.

'All right,' my brothers said and they forgot him.

But I did not forget my father. I have made up poems about him ever since.

These are some of those poems.

I call them raptors. I picked that word from a dictionary, with my eyes shut.

Toon Tellegen

I

My father
moved heaven and earth

heaven broke and the earth tore

my mother came running along a platform,
threw herself in front of a train on a daily basis

my father got out
and looked around, ill at ease
'what is that?'
        'what's left of heaven'
'and that abyss?'
        'that is in the earth, between yourself and everyone else'

he asked the station master
        what was still unattainable in life

my father felt so cold...

My father
searched for water,
his fingers raced about

my mother lay in bed
counted the strokes of her migraine,
my brothers ate bread and bacon
and reached for the stars

my father climbed onto the table,
'one drop!' he cried, 'just one drop!'

then he watered the wine with just one drop
and the wine seized him,
shook him,
wrung him out
and hung him up to dry, outside, on the clothes-line

my father was the world
and blew about in the wind

my brothers dreamed of cheese
                    and frivolous marmalade

my mother counted to a million.

My father
bit the dust –
my mother called him her maid,
                    her nimble chickabiddy,
drove him on

'do what she says,' said my brothers,
'if you want to save the world'

dust swirled up and drifted down,
everything that was imperishable perished

my brothers and my mother laughed, danced,
slipped through one another's fingers, buckled

and my father saved the world,
bit the dust.

My father
stuck to his guns

horses pushed their heads through windows,
girls took off their clothes, crawled through the eyes
of needles

my mother was a cloud, dissolved,
my brothers expired
in the wake of a benign kind of hunger
                             such as had never been observed

but my father stuck to his guns

and everyone who had nails, bit them,
eyes, cast them down

my father, my little father
grew like spearwort
out of his own skull.

My father
picked bitter fruits,
put them in his mouth

my brothers lifted him up,
'what should we do with him?' they asked,
my mother wept,
'shame him,' she said

my brothers shamed him,
my father shrank,
'and now?' my brothers asked,
'love him,' said my mother

and my brothers loved the bitter little father
in their hands.

My father
applied a double standard,
was Cain and Abel,
beat himself to death

my mother was already worm-eaten in those days
and my brothers were chickens born without heads

golden promises loomed on no horizon yet

my father cried:
'surely I am not my own keeper?'

'you are! you are!' the earth droned

my father buried himself,
the first dog eyed him with curiosity.

My father
got into deep water,
but my mother drowned

my brothers counted the crumbs on their plates,
my father had every ditch and pond filled in,
said he would not move an inch ever again

and his sorrow grew, glistened
until it became a palace with ballrooms and footmen
in black velvet liveries,
and with silver mirrors
that reflected the glow of his tears
and with balconies and windows
        from which he demanded silence
and called for feeling and forbearance,
and if need be, love…

my father grew old and the daylight
couldn't bear him any more.

My father
washed his hands in innocence

'what else should I wash them in?'
he asked
and he pitched my mother out of the window

'there!' he cried
and pitched my brothers out after her

but everyone called for my father,
demanded my father

my father was momentous and miserable
and he climbed into a vase
and wilted,
he was exhausted.

My father
was in the seventh heaven,
my mother visited him

she asked if she might kiss him,
my father said:
'that's what the other heavens are for'

they sat together in silence,
their hands in their laps,
there were begonias and cyclamen
and the smell of death

now and then an angel peered through a window
and asked if there was anyone who'd like to fight

my father shook his head,
my mother asked if she might continue to love him,
if only superficially and with reservation

doors creaked,
'hold it!' my father cried
and jumped up,
eternity was over

my brothers sat at table,
sadder than ever.

My father
stewed in his own juice –
my brothers put him on the table,
called my mother

'what's for supper?' she asked,
'our father,' they said, 'his heart and soggy soul,
may he taste delicious…!'

my father,
pathos descended on him,
blew its tin whistle
and cloaked him in nettles and slimy strings

hear him simmer,
see him steam

my mother serves him up.

My father
played with fire
and burst into flames

'it's only a game!' he cried,
while blazing high –
his flames licked at my mother

then he was burnt to cinders
and fluttered down

my brothers swept him up,
'this is serious now,' they said

my mother dusted off her clothes
and asked
how they wanted to remember him:
burning? smouldering? or in ashes?

but my brothers wanted to become awesome and alarming
and not remember anybody any more.

My father
became down and out

people rescued him
and showed him to my mother,
'this isn't him,' she said,
'this is someone else'

and she kissed that someone else
and begged him always to remain someone else

my father was a fish
that swam in the light
that vibrated round my mother,
swam into her eyes

my brothers lulled her to sleep
and my mother dreamed of summers
        and of the terrible nausea of existence.

My father
was on cloud nine

my brothers cried: 'what are you doing there?
what gave you the right?
did you not snatch our daily bread from us
just a minute ago?
is that what you're eating there now?'

'hush,' said my mother and she winced

'and your sins?' my brothers asked,
'they're still down here, what are we to do with them?
brush them up? commit them ourselves?'

they made a ladder
and climbed up to the clouds

and my father kissed them
and showed them temptations,
                each one more precious than the next

and he made it rain
and my mother fell ill.

My father
knew how to live,
he showed us how

and he keeled over, lay on the ground,
face down in the mud

'I *don't* know how to live,' he said,
'shall I show you *that*? I was mistaken!'
his voice broke

that day my brothers left the house,
my mother became a receptacle for aches and pains
and for stubborn suspicions of an ever mounting credibility,
my father lost
what remained of his usefulness.

My father
retraced his steps,
my mother watched him from afar

'now I am your friend again!' he exclaimed,
he climbed over a gate, jumped across a ditch,
walked into a meadow,
'and now your hero!'
and he lifted up the world,
'there's still nothing to it!'

then he fell,
he was very small, very well-groomed and very precise

and my mother stretched herself to the limit
and whispered:
'you may as well come here now.'

My father
twisted the facts

and the facts began to tear one by one,
my mother no longer existed,
my brothers woke up

my father took them fishing
and everything he was, he was not
                              and never would be again,
my brothers glistened,
gasped for air

then my father went on a journey,
my brothers helped him into his golden wings,
lifted him up and threw him into the air

and for a split second he was the sun, my sun,
that disappeared behind a cloud.

My father
wanted to alleviate suffering,
my mother approved,
and all the suffering in the world flowed towards him

my father alleviated it
and the suffering flowed back, burst its banks,
forced its way into houses,
rose to lips,
flowed up staircases, onto rooftops

and everyone who was still alive
embraced suffering,
cherished it
and loved it unconditionally

but my brothers taught each other how to gorge, how to kill
and how to be disgruntled,
suffering was beyond them.

My father
was a book

my brothers leafed through him,
pointed out the pictures to each other:
'look, here we are superfluous
and there our souls have been trodden on
and there, look, there it would have been better not to have existed!'

my mother did the laundry
and thought of men
who looked at her and asked her whether,
just for a brief moment,
they might think of her
and imagine taking off an item of her clothing

evening came
and my brothers leafed through my father more and more quickly,
discovered his indecipherability,
which explained their existence,
closed him, rested their heads on him
and fell asleep.

My father
was in the air, like a rumour,
like wildfire

my brothers stirred him up
so he could light up the world

and it grew hot and pressing
and my mother smouldered, caught fire

then my father fell on the ground,
changed his character and froze

and my brothers hacked a hole in him,
fished in him for comfort and resignation,
built houses on him, and little palaces

and my father spread
                    like restlessness and standoffishness
despite himself.

My father
sat on a mountain,
overlooked the world from there

'how small you are!' he called out to my mother,
'as if you don't exist!'
'and you,' he called out to the world, 'how insignificant you are!
as if you'll never matter again!'

no sign of my brothers anywhere

my father looked and looked
until his amazement wore off

then he made the mountain into a molehill,
with things that burrowed in the dark
and ferreted him out, every time he slept
while my mother got up
and sneaked away,
leaving him for good.

My father
created the world:
heaven and earth,
simplicity and ambivalence,
gluttony and shabbiness,
my brothers and their rage,
but not my mother

'she's not finished yet,' he would say
whenever the sun came up
which he had earmarked for the sky
and allowed to shine through curtains

and there was fighting in the streets and in the squares,
bad judgement was rampant,
false promises were made,
and there was dying and squandering

peace had to wait
until my mother was finished –
she lacked will.

My father
plucked up all his courage
and then flung it away

out of the corner of his eye he saw my mother and my brothers
gather up his courage
and give it to the down-hearted:
they knew that life was bygone, by the way, notwithstanding and
strange

the downhearted cheered, lifted each other up,
made sure their heads were in the clouds,
heard something grate, which they took to be the sun

and my father cast down his eyes
and plucked up all his sorrow

but he didn't know what to do with it

'just give it to me,' said my mother
and my father gave it to her.

My father
looked for injustice,
dug for it with his hands,
brought it to light

my brothers didn't believe him,
'injustice is bigger!' they cried
'injustice can also be small,' my father whispered,
'and gentle and sweet…
and something else too, I don't know…'

my father did nothing
he could not later regret,
cherished remorse and hankering
like priceless treasures,
wallowed in a sense of guilt
and fell down,
shattered my mother
and turned sour.

My father
tied himself into a thousand knots
and every knot became tighter and more inextricable,
and my mother kept unravelling him
and straightening him out

in those days my brothers went to school
with no clothes on,
'but not as a punishment!' they cried –
their teacher asked them if they were ashamed
and would rather be dead
or something like that,
'not today yet,' they said

it was winter, they shivered,
learned the weight of the world
and the difference between iron and lead
and between unsightly and dead,
went home again with no clothes on.

My father
abandoned all hope

my brothers handed him mortal fear
and raised his hands to heaven:
'now you may suffer,' they whispered, 'as intensely as you can'

oh my father, my green, worm-eaten father,
saint of liars, ignoramuses and the latter days…

my father suffered
and my mother wrapped her arms round him

my brothers turned into wolves,
            that looked for hunger,
found beauty
            in eternal worry.

My father
was speechless
like a dog that seems left for dead,
saw my mother sleeping

and never did a man tear apart a woman
with such tenderness, such meekness
and such bloodthirstiness on such a cold floor

in those days
my brothers carried the world on their shoulders,
cried: 'who wants the world... the whole world...
with all of heaven into the bargain...?'

'I do,' said my father
and he seized the world, sunk his teeth in the world

but the world was bitter
and my father spat it out.

My father
looked for a needle

'why not look for our mother,'
said my brothers,
they heard her sobbing

'I'm looking for her too,' said my father,
'and for peace and reconciliation,
but also for a needle'

'and us?' said my brothers,
'have you found us yet?'

'you're the hay,' said my father,
'how could I ever not find you?'

the heavens darkened,
unleashed their bitterness on the earth,
while my father found anguish and aloofness
and missed war by a hairbreadth.

My father
was wide of the mark

my brothers smiled,
wrote down every mishit in a notebook,
my mother did the laundry
or polished her nails

my father,
who kept himself alive with shame, regret and unease,
who threw in the towel on a daily basis,
who huffed and puffed
and was idle and in arrears,
who had nothing to say to anyone,
who was a spider with no web and no springtime,
who creaked and crunched, like an iron weathervane

one day he hit the mark
and my brothers threw him away.

My father
poured salt in wounds,
my father loved wounds,
kept making new, capriciously spreading wounds,
     ·   insidious wounds, undermining wounds,
looked in the attic for old and forgotten wounds,
beat them into my mother and my brothers,
filled them with salt and acid kisses

'happiness is a wound,' my father said, 'I'm looking for happiness'

my mother nodded,
pain is indispensable, she knew that.

My father
stayed out of the picture

it was summer,
my mother was being demolished,
my brothers broken down one by one

the sun was shining
and life became somehow unpleasant
and unmistakeably unspeakable –
no one knew what was the use of other people,
passers-by dragged superfluous love along

dust clouds lifted
and a house was built
made up of one maddening mother
                    and indeterminate brothers in abundance

and on the rocks,
                    lean and lost sight of,
my father
who stayed out of the picture.

My father
who rose and sank in esteem
saw my mother standing on the edge of a precipice

'I won't promise to save you,' he said
'no,'
'nor to make you happy or to live in peace with you,'
'oh no, not peace, and certainly not to live in,'
'nor that I will remember you even once,'
'no no, not remember, that never!' my mother still managed to echo

then my father turned round,
drank some vinegar
and walked on.

My father
screamed blue murder,
my mother made coffee

my father climbed onto chairs, tables,
leaned out of windows,
screamed calamity and intolerable pains,
screamed fire
and the approaching end of something unintelligible

my brothers kept their ears to the ground,
'listen!' they cried and jumped up,
'silence is approaching!'

they ran away, stumbled and fell
into barbed wire, complication and uncompromising principles

and my mother ran her hand
                    through my father's hair
and my father was silent.

My father
did not let sleeping dogs…
and they woke up and mauled him

my brothers looked on
and lulled the dogs back to sleep

'let *us* keep watch,' they said, 'we'll do the mauling'

the dogs dreamed
that they were beaten with great indifference
and left like lumber at low tide

my mother gathered up my father,
rinsed him clean,
glued him back together,
squeezed herself underneath him

didn't know what to do with his knees and his jaws

my brothers shrugged their shoulders,
they would have torn him to shreds.

II

My father
was in a terrible state –
'I know everything,' he said, 'I feel everything, I am everything…'

'that's enough now,' said my brothers
who were carrying him on their shoulders

'I hear everything, I see everything…' said my father

'that really is enough!' my brothers shouted,
flung him into a corner

'I think everything…' my father whispered

my brothers cursed him and ill-treated him,
their rage exceeded limits
that no one could imagine

I invent everything… my father still thought,
he closed his eyes,
just forget me.

My father
threw dust about

'that's the only thing,' he whispered to my mother,
'I can still do'

threw it in her eyes
and in the eyes of the angel with whom he was fighting,
while he had one hand under my mother's skirt

then he fell to the ground
and he got dust in his eyes

'now I don't know who you are any more,' he whispered,
my mother flung her arms round him

'name a hundred reasons,' my brothers cried,
'why you love him,
one reason why you're crying.'

My father
put on a show,
the sun shone and my brothers applauded

my father bowed
and disappeared offstage,
but he came back –
'now I shall die,' he said, 'and not just like that, at my leisure,
but gloriously and by storm,'
and he keeled over
and turned spectral and shadowy

my father played death and dreariness
and my mother shuddered,
I'm suffocating, she thought, now I'm suffocating,
or shall I do the laundry, or think up something practical?

and she lay on her back in the grass
and thought up a life without my father, without shame
and without sense.

My father
let a cup...
everyone held their breath,
that cup! that was meant for him!...
pass from him

no one had his knack for this

then my mother seized the cup,
my mother is so kind
          and so disarmingly inscrutable,
gave it to my brothers
who just happened to be busy tempting fate
on a paper ladder

my brothers began to roar with laughter,
drained the cup

and it rained that day,
not hard, but definitely for ever.

My father
kicked down doors,
found my mother,
let himself fall on top of her
and cried that he forgave himself
for everything that she lacked

my mother was silence
and the scent of wood and linen around him

my brothers approached hesitantly
and touched my father –
they couldn't help it –
'we feel so very moved now...' they said

from that day onward they were forever excluded
from touching, from innocence, from being moved

and my father got up
and asked them to suffer –
but in silence, like my mother –
or to be something that seems lost irretrievably,
just like everyone else.

My father
washed the dirty linen in public,
the neighbours watched

'the clean linen is inside,' my father said,
'it's made of passion and pure jealousy'

the neighbours nodded,
admired the dirtiness of the linen

my mother was inside,
dancing with cactuses and spiders,
the way only my mother could dance –
and yes yes… and yes yes…
my mother was young and luxuriant beyond measure,
but she dreamed of hunger,
grew scrawny and mute

my father threw mud at the linen,
washed it further afield,
washed it everywhere.

My father
let the fire run its course
and the world turned cold –
those who had still wanted to eliminate someone
warmed their hands

and the world turned blue
while people fanned it, stamped on it

my mother sewed thousands of buttons
onto thousands of coats

my brothers asked her questions about the last millimetre
between my father and everyone else

and the world turned black
and irreversible

my father slept,
my mother and my brothers were found
one winter morning
behind a fence,
the fire was dead.

My father
had the last word,
stored it in the dark
in the back of his mouth

it was a heavy word, a frightful word,
that pounded in his throat and throbbed
and uninterruptedly grew in significance

my brothers spoke of a hullabaloo and about bumps in their road
and my mother sang a song about pointless impatience
and half-hearted failing

my father bit his tongue,
shook his head, like a dog
that climbs out of the water
and wants to move on quickly,
cast down his eyes
and was dead.

My father
blew such a big trumpet
that he deafened everyone

then he blew the softest little trumpet,
its tune disappeared underground

my mother bent down and looked into the earth
to see if she might find him there

'yes yes,' said my brothers, 'that's where he must be,'
they spoke hurriedly,
invented his simplicity and amiability,
obscured his absurdity,
commended his delicate unforgettability,
stamped the soil down and prayed:
'may he be the last one to rise up
                in the hour of revelation'

my father cried:
'if I were to oversleep on *that* day, of all days...'
combed his hair by way of preparation.

My father
was a human being,
my mother and my brothers were something else

'something unfamiliar,' my father said,
'something unparalleled as yet,'
he pointed and sobbed,
cried out: 'roses! soap suds! over there!'
fell on his enormous trash-riddled knees before them,
kissed them –
they were so much bigger and more inscrutable than he could ever
        dare to pray to be even just once, for a single day

but they weren't human,
'I am human,' said my father,
'I alone.'

My father
destroyed things

people would come from far and wide,
would kneel before him,
give him the very last item they possessed
and my father would destroy it

my mother was wallpaper,
my brothers counted their ribs,
                    not one of which was missing

and everywhere the sun was shining
and philosophers dreamt inexplicable dreams,
wrote with trembling fingers in their godless notebooks:
'we have gathered this insight from all that exists:
there is always more, never less to be destroyed,
this is a law...'

and my father destroyed more and more things,
walked round in ever-increasing circles,
after all there was so much beauty...
and so much happiness too, love, irresistibility...

My father
was happy,
he had just become that

'don't touch!' he cried out to my mother

my brothers received his unhappiness –
'now you will never amount to anything, ever,' he said,
'no matter what'
and he pointed out attics to them
where they could shrivel up like sweet little apples
                                    or like spiders in their own webs

my father,
he radiated happiness, glowed, shone,
sparkled, excelled

'and what else?' he cried,
he danced on the table, embraced horses
        who, in his mind, fell to their knees,
'what else am I doing?'

my mother said nothing and went to a butcher's,
purchased headache, frozen shoulder and disgruntlement,
                            and oh yes, something gentle too,
did not return.

My father
soft-soaped the guilty
and they kissed each other and became innocent,
their guilt became liquid and disappeared

my mother flew up and shrivelled,
blew away in the wind, grinding her teeth

my brothers spoke of the extraordinary multiplication
of happiness
and of a sea of pure light and immensity

and the innocent kissed each other again and again,
without flagging

then my father grew scared to death,
his knees creaked,
his scent became monotonous

in nothing did he resemble everyday life,
he wept everyone into confusion

and the wind rose,
passers-by molested each other,
shuddered at the beauty of their confusion,
the toughness of their fears,
they lost their coherence,
cast off their shame
and walked on

and the innocent kissed each other and became more and
more innocent –
never were people more innocent,
neither in heaven, nor on earth

my father,
indistinguishable from death,
my world is his.

My father
was every bit
a man, a woman, a child

my brothers asked him
why my mother loved him
and why she kept kissing him gently,
kept killing him
and burying him
in the terrible moonlight

my father smiled
and told us about an accomplished peace,
an impetuous silence,
an enchanting messiah
and all the time in the world everywhere around him

and he spoke of a pin-head
that something fitted onto,
but he couldn't remember what.

My father
kept up appearances –
oh let everyone please keep them up!

but my brothers smashed them to pieces,
'we'd rather you kept us up,' they said

my father went on a journey
in search of even finer appearances
and in search of love and precision

but my mother stayed behind,
waited,
put my brothers in a box,
drilled holes in it
      so that they could peer at the stars at night,
whispered something encouraging to them,
threw away the key.

My father
acted in good faith and took the smooth,
my mother blushed and took the rough

my brothers were allowed to choose,
chose my mother

my father stayed alone,
made notches in the walls round him,
and he became dull and out of date
and the smooth crumbled,
became uncertain

but my father just managed to hang onto
one last scrap of certainty

and that scrap was everything,
the famous everything,
of which there was no more.

My father
looked for someone, just one person,
who was different from himself –
looked in the nooks and crannies
                between heaven and earth,
fell to his knees, again and again,
and cried:
'oh, let there be one person
who is not like me!'

magpies screeched in overwhelming sycamores
and outcasts fled the remnants of their own shadow,
millions and millions of them

but there was no one
who did not fall to his knees
and did not beg for someone,
one someone,
who was not like him.

My father
slept
and my mother bent over him
and said: 'look, he is unaware of any harm'

my brothers didn't hear her,
spat on each other, despised each other,
brought each other to a majestic and mysterious kind
        of rack and ruin

my father awoke
and there were mosquitoes, wasps, tiny hyenas, little vultures
and one fly, one small fly,
and my father stretched out
and said: 'ah, little fly, what are *you* doing here...'
and swatted it.

My father
dragged things by the hair,
sawed, chafed,
hit nails on the head

my mother lay at his feet,
searched for her feelings,
'where are those dumb feelings now...'

at the windows sensitive girls
who were weeping uncontrollably,
dreaming of a life without doubt
                          and improbability

then my mother found
one tiny trampled down tender little feeling

but it wasn't large enough
                          to love somebody with,
and she sat down to weep a little

my brothers were things
with a grain of sense.

My father
was in a tight corner

he couldn't move in any direction

he called for my mother,
but my mother wasn't there,
he called for my brothers,
but my brothers weren't there

he wrenched and wrenched
until he was exhausted

then he flew away, waved in passing at my mother
and my brothers,
who for the thousandth time just
                    happened to appear out of thin air

oh consciousness of guilt, steaming and in dishes,
in the middle of the table,
my father,
he almost wanted to die.

My father,
who blows up rocks, blows away people, blows out peace,
blows off simplicity,
cried out that he was cold and despondent
and that if *he* wasn't saved…

my mother stood still,
torn between aversion and mercy,
wrung her hands,
tied inextricable knots in her thoughts –
dreaming of a little Alexander –
and called my brothers

but my brothers were in their millions,
were tired of saving.

My father
looked in a mirror

'get out of my sight,'
he said softly, almost inaudibly,
and he vanished from his sight

my mother and my brothers danced, clumsily
                              and apparently superfluously,
out of joyless joy, for years,
thinking about everything they did not miss

then my father grew pale and heartrending,
looked in dozens of mirrors,
bent over lakes and rivers,
peeked through windows,
accosted everyone in the street

but he couldn't find himself any more.

My father
thanked my mother
        who was ashen and inadequate,
thanked a poppy and some refuse at the side of the road,
thanked underlying principles idols adversity,
thanked words that fell into his lap,
thanked my brothers who asked him
        if they might despise him from the bottom of their hearts,
and the sun went down,
and my father thanked himself,
        fell on his knees for himself,
thanked himself in the name of heaven and earth: the dross
        that he fell into
                and made himself comfortable in,
my father was so gratuitous...

My father
was immense and limitless

it was raining
and my brothers were horses
that trotted
across the vastness of my father –
'there's no end to you!' they cried out
and sank into the mud
            of his insatiable hunger

my mother thought about them,
my mother could think so beautifully,
            so without frills and roundaboutness,
my mother dwelt on everyone

the sun appeared,
lit up idylls and oblivion
and my father was eternity

but my mother is here, now,
            a fraction of every second.

My father
made things hot for people,
set fire to the senseless ones
                who drag kingdoms about,
and they spread in all directions,
scorching the world

nothing senseless escaped my father's notice

my father was a human being
the way wolves and valleys are human beings,
                and the sun and a clear sky

my mother and my brothers asked him
how they should live

my father demonstrated it to them
and they lived more and more sensibly
until they grew mature and misshapen

then my father thought up something new,
something paltry,
and called it perfect.

My father –
how fathomless was the depth of his shame –
he woke up
and struck my mother,
struck my brothers
struck women who gathered round him

his hands were on fire

and my mother got up
and asked him how he had slept –
undoubtedly miraculously –
and my brothers got up,
dressed him and placed him at the table,
and all the women got up,
crept under his clothes,
whispered and lisped,
examined the downiness of his silence,
and my father felt ashamed
and struck himself.

My father,
there was a gaping hole in him
in which my mother and my brothers
entertained themselves

they sat at table,
they laughed, played dice
and cheated

and the hole in my father grew bigger
and bigger,
and shots were fired in my father,
people screamed
            and were arrested

a car stopped on the edge
of my father,
my mother and my brothers got in

'nothing more will ever be heard of you,'
said the driver and touched his cap

grass grew in my father,
there was a stench in my father,
something was howling
full stop.

My father
looked for love

when he found it,
          he declared it complicated,
made it simple,
polished it, cut it
                    until it was smooth and nondescript
and fitted everyone

at night he studied my mother and my brothers,
captured them in formulae,
factorised them, made them cancel each other out,
raised them to dizzying powers,
dissected their desires,
examined them under a microscope,
described them, ordered them,
recorded their destiny

while he was looking for love.

My father
was a mistake
of a painful and irreparable kind,
and he asked my mother to blame him
for being nonetheless human

my mother nodded and wanted to cause him harm, scarcity
                                          and long-lasting ineptitude,
but she didn't know how
and she forgave him, caressed him

sincerity will split the world,
senseless offenders will dance on their graves

my mother grew old and indirect
and my father edged his way out of her mind

my father,
she should have hated him,
she ate crumbs out of his hand.

My father
died a thousand deaths,
my mother put on a brave face,
my brothers were lost for words

my father,
a lonely dead man among countless immortals,
no one died as often, as daily and as disastrously
as he did

and those who saw him die became uneasy
                              and awkward,
wanted to make up for it, make up for something,
didn't know what or how

and every time my brothers would be lost for words again,
would say: 'but…' and 'you…' and 'that…',
my father would die all over again
and my mother would put on a brave face,
                              hair-raisingly brave.

My father
couldn't comprehend himself any more,
became grey and agitated,
was turning to dust

my mother and my brothers hated dust
and wondered
why he didn't turn into something else,
something other than that eternal dust
which even the deadest dead were mortally sick of –
why not into light,
why did he not find his way into rooms, basements, winters,
                                 the very heart of things, delirious,
why not make people sing,
think...?

and they burst into a sad coughing,
cast down their eyes.

III

My father
and then for hours, days
nothing
and then my mother, trudging along, lugging his suffering,
          spilling some of it now and then
(but with such gentle eyes, she)
and then my brothers, angry,
steaming mad,
dense clouds came off them,
and then nothing again
for months, years
and then my father again
– 'where are you all?' –
old and hurried,
nobody beside him,
                    behind him,
nobody any more.

My father
fished for answers,
found none,
but he sang

real fishermen float in silence, crowned with glory,
with their bellies up, like chairmen of boards
drifting out to sea

my father sang about patient endurance
and about hunger that gnawed at him,
wanted something of him,
refused to tell him what it was

grinding his teeth while he sang softly

and my mother heard him
and took him with her –
didn't tell him where –
pushed him gently backwards on a bed,
nestled herself on top of him

and they became entangled
in the space that stretched beyond the furthest stars
                              and induced the deepest sleep,
the great slovenly unknown.

My father
was everywhere,
but not where everyone thought
   they had found him at last

'*there! there* he is!'
the world buzzed,
everyone pointed at him,
recognised him, overwhelmed him, wrapped arms
                                   round him

my brothers glowed and nodded:
'yes, that's him... *that* is him...'

my mother closed her eyes,
felt his peculiar messy nearness,
his half-hearted fingers,
his misplaced lips,
whispered his name:

– my father was everywhere, always,
but not there, not then, that time, that one time –

'my dearest love.'

My father
slept through headaches, hazards and uncontrollable
                              feelings of inferiority,
slept through my mother,
slept through unrest and sorrow

my father established a wilderness of sleep
                              and inevitable fatigue,
slept my brothers to the end of his tether,
                              floating gently in the wind,
coldly and maliciously slept the light out of his face,
slept pity to death

my father slept with all summers, winters,
                              slept with the tide,
wrapped girls, dogs round him in his sleep

sparrows howled, swallows blared,
heaven and earth shook him, spat on him,
growled in his colossal, incredibly sharp ears

but my father slept
                  like a thousand logs
in the moonlight
on the banks of a river.

My father
was gone,
but not really

my mother and my brothers fumbled
                          with their insecurity, unflagging,
muttered:
'he's gone forever'
but he wasn't really gone for ever,
'he's gone completely'
but he wasn't really gone completely,
'he's gone irrevocably'
but he wasn't really gone irrevocably

even the realest thing
                is not the very realest thing

darkness fell, thrushes sang in trees
                          of dubious charm,
and everything uninhabited became even more uninhabited,
but my father,
my tiny, tiny, irrelevant father,
was not quite really, really gone.

My father
explained himself

my mother took leave of her senses
and my brothers sought refuge in relative things,
                    matchsticks, yarn, washing-up liquid

it was a fine day
and my father tried
        with all the means at his disposal
                to love truly and genuinely,
                        and love no less than everyone,
stood on his toes,
bit his nails,
held his breath…

but my mother and my brothers
                        were open to only one explanation
and then no more,
and evening came
and my father whispered: 'reign of terror, reign of terror…'

My father,
behold the tears of my father,
behold his sorrow,
    his hunger for simplicity and harmony,
behold his thinking,
    his principles in long rows, each waiting its turn,
    his opinions, whirling round, nauseous and elated,
    his suspicions, wrong, wrong, wrong,
behold also the sun
    that keeps rising and rising
    and never sets,
behold moral dilemmas,
    behold them pass, murmuring, whispering, going nowhere,
and my father got up
and became immoral.

My father
choked on his daily bread
and on his millions of debtors

wherever he went
my brothers crackled under his feet,
wherever he slept
forgiveness dangled gently in the wind

he kissed my mother
                    in the shadow of the hereafter,
fumbling with the angry buttons of her soul,
and my mother exclaimed:
'what are you doing? why are you kissing me?
why don't you give me a kingdom? now and here!
oh please…!'

but my father said amen,
he gave nothing,
he is one of us.

My father
created pain,
clothed it in my mother

and my mother fought with the pain,
dug her nails into the pain,
and the pain inflamed her,
grew attached to her

then my father created misconceptions
                and reductions ad absurdum,
wrote them down on bits of paper, pinned them on walls
and went fishing,
did not come back

and angels sang in the pain,
dust particles danced in the pain,
children tossed the pain high up into the air,
and when someone dies
he turns into pain

and my father created mud
and melancholy
and the passing of people
                and a measure of sadness.

My father
bowed to the inevitable
and my mother slept with him,
wept over the incomprehensible
        and the great all-embracing improbable

morning came
and my brothers saw her tears,
set fire to my father

and the inevitable rose from his ashes,
with dignity and mercy,
blowing kisses and casting meaningful glances,
whilst tripping over its own inevitability from time to time

and silence came
and unenlightenment – of a transparent kind –
and those who knew something nodded their heads

my mother slowly slept her way downstream
from upland plains.

My father
talked gibberish
and gibberish fled into my mother

oh my father,
my bright, sun-baked father,
        seasoned by infidelity and idle days,
my rusty, conniving father
        who creaks and crunches and opens:
no one at home,
no one to forgive a faux pas,
my adorable brothers, caught in a black frame,
and all that remains for us:
a note on the table:

        I'm gone,
        don't forget to live or whatever

my father bawled gibberish, begged gibberish,
but my mother kept silent
                and caressed him.

My father
racked his brains
over the difference between pure and mixed feelings

my brothers jumped up and asked:
'is it racking itself to death, that brain of yours,
what do you think,
should we commit you to the earth
and devote a few last tears to you,
or should we step over you
and depart,
allow time to pass
and return, like lost sons,
in gigantic swarms,
dark and dishevelled,
but too late…?'

my mother was a train
that departed punctual to the minute
and derailed by the book

my father hallowed her name.

My father
was already himself,
my mother was still a young girl,
my brothers so very unborn
                that they sparkled in the sun

'are you coming…' my mother asked,
she was wearing red shoes
                    and her mother's corals,
she had glitters on her nails
                    and in her long red hair,
but dumbness struck my father,
chased him away

stalks snapped, frogs blew themselves up
and everything that shone evaporated

it was May
and my father didn't know that he would never be anyone
but himself,
and that he lacked something,
something painful,
something invaluable of no consequence

and that summer was in the air,
and something misleading,
over and over again.

My father
promised everything, pledged everything –
'even love?' my mother asked –
'everything' –
'even, even...' she searched for a word
that was greater than happiness –
'everything!' my father cried, 'or don't you know
what everything is?'
and he gave her everything
and my mother burnt down

then my father walked across seas and oceans,
his voice echoed by the earth's aversion,
the stiffness of the years

he was still thinking, he cried
about dissolution and syrup!
'patience! patience!'

and he promised a golden spider in a golden web
and billions of golden flies of a devastating short-sightedness
in the radiant dawn of insanity

my father was so alone...

My father
was nobody

my mother had geraniums blossoming
                on every window sill, every balcony,
rarely said a word
and when darkness fell she lay down beside nobody,
felt nobody's lips on her lips

but the nights grew tired, took their leave of her,
let her slide,
'will you be coming back?' my mother asked,
but the nights no longer heard her,
nights are deaf and self-absorbed

my mother tried to be courageous and quiet
and to resemble a swan and an azalea too,
nobody showed her the truth

and my brothers looked for her, called for her,
every morning afresh

but nobody woke her up,
nobody's voice, nobody's scent,
        nobody's deepest desire even,
and my mother called back:
'she? she's not here.'

My father
is a tiny bit – one millionth – deader
than dead

everyone is dead
every dog rat canary is dead
my brothers are dead
my mother is irresistibly mournfully dead
                              like a dry stick in a stubble field
accidental passers-by are dead
onlookers intruders and orphans
there's a rush on death
those most irrevocably dead grumble
people die falsely messily mumbling fumbling
perish illegally quickly quickly
longevity strictly prohibited
away with life-saving! away with long suffering!
notions about resurrection banned willy-nilly!
mourning must be done more efficiently!
no more than one item of clothing torn to pieces!
best wishes tempered drastically! condolences discarded!
no more courage of despair! no agony no last gasp!
the toughest last straw severed!
'ow did you want 'im laid out?
cold!
and everywhere
along long forgotten streets and under old
                              befuddled street lamps
are the dead that coo
chant chirpy songs of lamentation
and want to speak no ill know no ill
revelations are needed! now!
all daffodils carnations dandelions are suffocating
all that is lovely and ghastly everything
everything is dead

but my father is deader
just a little deader
my tiny painstaking father
keeper of my grace.

My father
begot surprise

and surprise begot my mother and my brothers,
they peered at each other,
nodded at each other cautiously
and began to dance,
first slowly, but then faster and faster,
they whirled round
and begot cheerfulness, exuberance
and fields full of poppies, cornflowers,
picked armfuls

but exuberance begot habitualness,
habitualness begot lethargy
and lethargy begot reluctance –
the sun went down
and reluctance begot dislike and disgust,
          dressed in their uncomfortable, washed out coats,
and disgust wanted to beget death

but how do you beget death?

My father
didn't waste his breath
                on my mother and my brothers,
held himself aloof from affection
                and comforting gestures

my father put a spoke
                in every wheel that turned

but my father was also flimsy as a rope of sand
and leaky as a sieve,
spent like water,
good for nothing
and to no one's surprise
                more utterly inferior than average

and the heavens opened,
angels flew up and down, trumpeting with gusto
and a Despairing Voice cried:
'who are you, but who *are* you?'

and my father looked up
and said:
'not the least of men.'

My father
wanted to love my mother,
wanted nothing more profoundly than that

and he gave her innocence and unpredictability
and fine promises
        that she had to live up to,
but it was not enough

then he gave her my brothers
and fistfuls of down-and-outs and charitableness
and – for lack of anything better –
melancholy and meaningful boredom,
but it was still never enough

my father didn't know what more he could do,
he wanted so badly to love her...

and he bent over her
and gave her rain
and inconsolability
and relentless nights

and he loved her.

My father
got under the skin
                of the placid,
invented subterfuge and self-deception,
destroyed consciences

my mother and my brothers wept
(they cursed, spat and shouted,
but they called it weeping)

and evening came
and my father collected giggling young girls
who caused little mishaps –
'oh sorry! sorry!' they sobbed
and tumbled into his arms –
and he made an end to assumptions
about his true nature

my father was a crow
who was nevertheless incorruptible,
perched on pitch-black branches
and croaked: 'corrupt me! corrupt me!'
and who was wizened
and without faith
and underexposed
and who fizzled out
one day.

My father
was at his wits' end,
'I am!' he cried, 'I really am!'

my mother wanted to be that too,
but didn't know how,
stood in front of mirrors, tried on dress after dress,
stockings, hairpins

'you have to lose heart,' said my father,
'you have to speak ill of yourself'

'you're nearly there,' said my brothers
and recommended a new kind of headache to her,
                          one that rapidly consumes you,
and an ungovernable hunger

my father slept at his wits' end,
danced at his wits' end

my mother lived in vain.

My father
buried his head,
his unenlightened soul-destroying bloody-minded head,
in the vast arid ill-fated sand churned up by my mother –
my brothers held onto his feet

thus he warned the world, for the last time!

and the world nodded –
the world wasn't daft, it too craved happiness
                                        and bliss –
and ceased to exist

then my father was alone,
built a small rickety castle
and gave birth to an elephant
        which he called Finicky.

My father
found happiness,
the way children find it, outside, in the street,
                    when everyone's still asleep

my brothers seized him, beat him,
ripped off his clothes,
'where is it?' they shouted

my father shook his head,
'it's safe with me,' he said,
'only with me'

he bled,
the way horses bleed in a gleaming slaughterhouse
with water running down the walls
                    and dizzying terms of employment,
crawled slowly, moaning softly, but happily,
out of their sight.

My father
saw ghosts
and ghosts saw him –
'funny fellow!' they called out, delighted,
and crept into his head,
discovered ambition and small depraved desires
and dust everywhere, so much dust, everywhere…
tapped against his ears,
peered through his eyes,
saw a world
          that is unthinkable,
looked inside again,
saw feverish fabrications,
heard girls singing
      about flowers that wilt blithely
      and about ships that dance on the waves
      and go down in style

my mother and my brothers sat at table,
cut each other up.

My father
was so small,
so utterly senselessly irreparably small,
but no one asked him to become bigger and have more sense

my mother stroked him and clasped him in her arms,
my brothers asked themselves
whether they had ever wondered about him

my father,
inventor of miserliness and thoughtlessness,
rolled up his cosmic sleevelets

sparrows chirped in gutters and in hedges,
dew shimmered on wobbly cobwebs

and my father spat on the earth – tiny, lucid splodges –
and attacked heaven – little slaps, little kicks –
but no one asked him to call it a day
and become visible, divisible and considerable

my father, my paltry father,
my little Goliath.

(My father
quite honestly, really wanted only one thing:
to be small and grubby

and he was small and unimaginably grubby,
grinned bitterly: 'I, I, I...'

my mother heard him, swept him up
and threw him away,
and she said to my brothers:
'that was all.')

My father
didn't know that he was in despair,
it was his blind spot

my mother asked him: 'why are you sighing like that?'
'I am sighing out of happiness,' he said,
'but why do you look so sad then?'
'I am thinking of something beautiful,'
my father never doubted
                    the truthfulness of his feelings

the sun went down
and he threw himself in front of a train,
cried that he was playing with my brothers

and it grew murky and miserable
around him

my father knew himself,
knew everything about himself

but not that he was in despair.

My father
smashed rocks, smashed mud,
smashed glass darkness face to face

my mother let her tears roll quietly,
my brothers shouted and became too much for everyone,
went to sea,
gambled away their minds
and were passed on to the waves

then my father
        who encompassed everything and saw everything,
smashed the dust
        that lay on his life,
smashed it until it whirled and danced for him

and he looked in a mirror obstinately
and screamed
until he became poignant.

My father
was in safe hands, was extolled to the skies,
but hands wither
and my father fell to the ground

my father lay on the ground
and invented one person
who invented him who lay on the ground
and was alone

one person who was indescribable
                              and had big, sovereign hands
and drove a wedge into pride and indifference

and the moon came up
and my father growled a final something
and was dead.

My father
was coming to an end,
overflowed the banks of his will

my mother let him ripple, surge,
and my brothers set their course by him,
rocked on the long waves
                    of his decline,
fished for the secrets
                    he no longer possessed,
let him think,
let him be unable to put anything into words

evening came
and his sun let itself go under in him,
let him grow cold and remote,
his storms died down
and his winter beckoned to him: here! here!

but my father was asleep –
his gulls were tired
and settled on him.

My father
began to confuse things
      for want of people, thoughts

my mother embraced him,
took things away from him

then he was left with my brothers,
but they were growing twisted and entangled
till they became one single brother of no significance at all

then he opened himself
and elephants appeared, and white doves, ants, irises
               in the chinks of his mind,
but not for long,
my mother closed him again

and it turned cold
and my father was like a lamb
           for want of death.

My father
was something
no one could put their finger on

nice, said my mother,
but he wasn't nice,
brave, everything,
but he wasn't brave and not everything either

gone, said my brothers, unmistakeable, inconceivable,
inconvenient...

they rubbed their hands:
'we'll get to the bottom of it,' they cried,
'don't worry!'...

sad, people said who didn't know him,
but he wasn't sad,
alone,
but he wasn't alone,
everybody,
nor everybody nor large nor shy
nor a crying shame

and the sun went down,
blackbirds were singing,
        but so beautifully and so naturally...
and spring came
and my father pointed at me.

My mother stood in the doorway,
she stood there in a blue dress with a red waistband,
her hair was tousled,
my brothers called out for her to come inside

my mother always did what they asked,
but she no longer knew what was inside
and what outside

she went outside,
this is inside, she thought, this must be inside,
everyone is here

it was a fine day
and everyone was there, everyone, everyone,
she took a deep breath
and didn't think of my father

I thought you were always thinking of him, she thought,
yes, but now I am not thinking of him

everyone loved her, that was obvious,
and loved her more and more, more wildly, more hungrily

how odd, my mother thought,
why do they do that,
she cast down her eyes

and my brothers called her again,
slammed their fists on the table,
plates bounced up, glasses toppled over

and my mother went inside
and thought of my father,
spring had come, and no mercy.